Pop! Pop! Pop!

by Christina Miller

illustrated by Nicole Wong

Target Skill Short Oo/o/
High-Frequency Words *they, you, of*

PEARSON

Scott
Foresman

Pam, Tim, and Ron have a kit.

It is a flower kit.

The kids and Mom look in the kit.

Can you look in the kit?

Ron can see a pot in the kit.

Pam can see a mat in the kit.

Tim can see seeds in the kit.

They fit the mat on the table.
The kids drop dirt in the pot.

Pam, Tim, Ron, and Mom
tap seeds in the pot.

Look! They can see a pot of flowers.
Pop, pop, pop!